1 6 MAY 2014

2 3 JAN 2015

- 1 SEP 2015

H H

2 0 FEB 2015

0 6 JUL 2018

2 2 AUG 2015

Richmond upon Thames Libraries

online at www.richmond.gov.uk/libraries

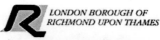

LONDON BOROUGH OF
RICHMOND UPON THAMES

Michael Hurley

9071 0 000 165 872

D1549998

Raintree is an imprint of Capstone Global Library
Limited, a company incorporated in England and
Wales having its registered office at 7 Pilgrim Street,
London, EC4V 6LB – Registered company number:
6695582

www.raintreepublishers.co.uk
myorders@raintreepublishers.co.uk

Text © Capstone Global Library Limited 2014
First published in hardback in 2014
Paperback edition first published in 2014
The moral rights of the proprietor have been
asserted.

All rights reserved. No part of this publication
may be reproduced in any form or by any means
(including photocopying or storing it in any medium
by electronic means and whether or not transiently
or incidentally to some other use of this publication)
without the written permission of the copyright
owner, except in accordance with the provisions
of the Copyright, Designs, and Patents Act 1988 or
under the terms of a licence issued by the Copyright
Licensing Agency, Saffron House, 6–10 Kirby Street,
London EC1N 8TS (www.cla.co.uk). Applications for
the copyright owner's written permission should be
addressed to the publisher.

Edited by Claire Throp and Vaarunika Dharmapala
Designed by Joanna Hinton-Malivoire
Picture research by Hannah Taylor
Originated by Capstone Global Library Limited
Printed and bound in China by Leo Paper Products

ISBN 978 1 406 26625 2 (hardback)
17 16 15 14 13
10 9 8 7 6 5 4 3 2 1

ISBN 978 1 406 26630 6 (paperback)
17 16 15 14 13
10 9 8 7 6 5 4 3 2 1

British Library Cataloguing in Publication
Hurley, Michael.
A-Z of the World Cup. -- (World Cup fever)
796.3'34-dc23
A full catalogue record for this book is available
the British Library.

Acknowledgements
We would like to thank the following for permission
to reproduce photographs: Alamy Images p. 29 (©
Robert Harding World Imagery); Corbis pp. 5 (Gerard
Rancinan; Pierre Perrin/Sygma), 17 (EPA/Marcus
Brandt), 23 (Frank Kleefeldt/DPA), 25 (Stephane
Reix/For Picture), 42 (TempSport/Christian Liewig),
43 (TempSport/Jerome Prevost); Getty Images pp.
11 (Franck Fife/AFP), 13 bottom (Laurence Griffiths),
14 (Cameron Spencer), 15 (Lalo Yasky/WireImage),
16 (Vanderlei Almeida/AFP), 20 (Lars Baron), 24
(Shaun Botterill – FIFA), 27 (David Cannon/Allsport),
30 (Alexander Heimann), 33 & 36 (Bob Thomas),
34 (AFP Photo/Jewel Samad), 35 (Popperfoto), 40
(Steve Haag); Photoshot pp. 4 (Wolfgang Weihs), 6,
10 (Picture Alliance/DPA), 13 top (Picture Alliance/
Sven Simon), 18 (Picture Alliance), 32 (Alexander
Sandvoss), 37 (Picture Alliance/Ralf Hirschberger),
39 (DPA/Oliver Berg), 41; Press Association pp. 8, 9,
19 & 26 (Empics), 31 (AP Photo), 38.

All background images courtesy of Shutterstock.

Cover photograph of a football displaying the flags of
South American footballing nations reproduced with
permission of Getty Images (Ian McKinnell).

Every effort has been made to contact copyright
holders of material reproduced in this book. Any
omissions will be rectified in subsequent printings if
notice is given to the publisher.

Disclaimer
All the internet addresses (URLs) given in this book
were valid at the time of going to press. However,
due to the dynamic nature of the internet, some
addresses may have changed, or sites may have
changed or ceased to exist since publication. While
the author and publisher regret any inconvenience
this may cause readers, no responsibility for any such

**London Borough of Richmond
Upon Thames**

RTHAH   DISCARDED

90710 000 165 872

Askews & Holts	
J796.334 HUR JUNIOR N	£8.99
	9781406266306

CONTENTS

A IS FOR...

AFRICAN REPRESENTATION

The African continent was first represented at the FIFA World Cup in 1934 when Egypt played at the tournament. Since Morocco qualified in 1970, 12 other teams from Africa have played at the World Cup, including Senegal, Côte d'Ivoire, and South Africa. Cameroon has the best record of any of these countries at the World Cup, and has appeared at six tournaments.

ARGENTINA

Argentina has a very good record at the World Cup, and was one of the original teams that took part in the first tournament in 1930. Argentina reached the final but was beaten 4–2 by the hosts, Uruguay. In 1978 Argentina hosted the World Cup when it was played on the South American continent for the fourth time. Argentina won the 1978 World Cup (see below), beating the Netherlands 3–1 in the final in Buenos Aires. Argentina won its second World Cup trophy in 1986 when star player Diego Maradona led the team to success with his outstanding individual performances and amazing skills.

AZTECA STADIUM

The Azteca Stadium in Mexico (see above) is one of the most famous and historic venues in World Cup history. The Azteca has hosted many great World Cup matches, and fans here have witnessed some great goals and several controversial moments. This Mexican landmark was built for both the 1968 Olympic Games and the 1970 World Cup, where it was the venue for the final. In the 1970 final, Brazil triumphed with a convincing 4–1 win over Italy.

DID YOU KNOW?

The Azteca is the only stadium to have hosted two World Cup finals, in 1970 and 1986.

B IS FOR...

BRAZIL

Brazil is the most successful country ever to have taken part in the World Cup. The Brazilian team has entered and qualified for every tournament since it started in 1930, and has won the World Cup a record five times. Their most recent success came in 2002 when they beat Germany 2–0 in the final.

BRAZIL'S WORLD CUP WINS		
YEAR	**OPPONENT**	**SCORE**
1958	SWEDEN	5–2
1962	CZECHOSLOVAKIA	3–1
1970	ITALY	4–1
1994	ITALY	0–0 3–2 on penalties
2002	GERMANY	2–0

▲ Brazilian legends Pelé (centre) and Ronaldo share a joke.

This map shows Brazil and the surrounding countries. Brazil covers nearly half the continent of South America.

WORLD CUP HOSTS

Brazil was chosen by FIFA as the venue for the 2014 World Cup. It is the second time that Brazil has hosted the tournament. When Brazil hosted the World Cup in 1950, the team made it all the way to the final. The excitement and anticipation surrounding that match was incredible, and more than 173,000 fans flocked to the Maracana Stadium (see page 22) in Rio de Janeiro to watch their team. After taking the lead, Brazil was beaten 2–1 by Uruguay in the final. The Brazilian players and fans were devastated.

FANTASTIC VENUES

Brazilian sports fans are very passionate about football and their football team. New stadiums have been specially built for the 2014 World Cup, and these fantastic venues will be full of colour and noise when the tournament kicks off.

DID YOU KNOW?

The official football that will be used at the 2014 World Cup is called the "Brazuka". A poll of Brazilian fans was taken to choose the name, which reflects national pride in the Brazilian way of life.

C IS FOR...

CHINA

China is the fourth largest country in the world and has the world's largest population (more than 1.3 billion people). However, China has only once qualified for the World Cup, in 2002, when the World Cup was co-hosted by neighbouring countries, Japan and South Korea (see page 21).

FUTURE WORLD CUP SUCCESS?

China has started to attract famous, top-class players from other countries to appear in their Chinese League. The Chinese footballers hope to learn from these more experienced foreign players and improve their game enough to become regular World Cup qualifiers in the future.

CONCACAF, CONMEBOL, AND CAF

Each area of the world is separated by FIFA into six different regions. Teams from these regions play each other to qualify for the World Cup.

CONCACAF stands for the Confederation of North, Central American, and Caribbean Association Football. The United States and Mexico are in this region.

CONMEBOL stands for Confederación Sudamericana de Fútbol. Brazil and Argentina are in this region.

CAF stands for Confédération Africaine de Football. This confederation contains all the countries in Africa.

The other FIFA regions are UEFA (Europe), AFC (Asia), and OFC (Oceania).

D IS FOR...

DANISH DYNAMITE

The Danish team made their debut at the 1986 World Cup – and became the talk of the tournament. Wearing their distinctive red and white shirts, the young and talented team produced some stunning performances with their attractive and attacking football style.

HIGHS AND LOWS

Denmark won all three group matches convincingly, but were badly beaten 5–1 by Spain in their second-round match. Denmark had led 1–0 until just before half-time, when a mistake allowed Spain to score an easy equalizer. Denmark pushed hard in the second half to retake the lead, but their style was too offensive and Spain scored four more goals on the counter-attack. The Denmark players were devastated, but they had entertained fans all over the world with some fantastic football.

DID YOU KNOW?

The 1986 Denmark team is the only team since 1950 to both score and concede five or more goals in matches at the same World Cup.

E IS FOR...

ENGLAND, AND 1966

The 1966 World Cup was hosted by England, and the English team reached the final – beating West Germany 4–2. Geoff Hurst (see below, right) scored a hat-trick, or three goals, and became the first player to do so in a World Cup final. In the 11 finals since 1966, Geoff Hurst's record is yet to be matched or beaten.

DISAPPOINTING RECORD SINCE '66

England has qualified for eight World Cups since winning the tournament in 1966. However, the closest England has come to repeating their magnificent victory since then has been one semi-final match in Italy, in 1990. England lost that match against West Germany in a penalty shoot-out.

▼ Patrice Evra (far left) walks away from his teammates and his manager during the 2010 World Cup.

EVRA LEADS A REVOLT

At the 2010 World Cup in South Africa, the behaviour of the French team shocked fans all over the world. The French striker Nicolas Anelka reacted badly after a defeat by Mexico and insulted the France manager. He was sent home for his actions. The other French players disagreed with this and the team captain, Patrice Evra, led a revolt that included the squad refusing to train during the tournament. Evra was also seen arguing face-to-face with one of the French coaches. As a punishment for his behaviour, Evra was dropped from the team for their vital last group match against South Africa. France lost the match 2–1, and the team exited the tournament in disgrace.

F IS FOR...

WORLD CUP FINAL RESULTS SINCE THE START OF THE TOURNAMENT	
1930	URUGUAY 4–2 ARGENTINA
1934	ITALY 2–1 CZECHOSLOVAKIA
1938*	ITALY 4–2 HUNGARY
1950	URUGUAY 2–1 BRAZIL
1954	WEST GERMANY 3–2 HUNGARY
1958	BRAZIL 5–2 SWEDEN
1962	BRAZIL 3–1 CZECHOSLOVAKIA
1966	ENGLAND 4–2 WEST GERMANY
1970	BRAZIL 4–1 ITALY
1974	WEST GERMANY 2–1 THE NETHERLANDS
1978	ARGENTINA 3–1 THE NETHERLANDS
1982	ITALY 3–1 WEST GERMANY
1986	ARGENTINA 3–2 WEST GERMANY
1990	WEST GERMANY 1–0 ARGENTINA
1994	BRAZIL 0–0 ITALY [Brazil won 3-2 in a penalty shoot-out]
1998	FRANCE 3–0 BRAZIL
2002	BRAZIL 2–0 GERMANY
2006	ITALY 1–1 FRANCE [Italy won 5-3 in a penalty shoot-out]
2010	SPAIN 1–0 HOLLAND

FINALS

The World Cup final is one of the most popular sporting events in the world. In 2010 almost 700 million people around the world watched the final between Spain and the Netherlands. Spain scored with only a few minutes of the match left, and won the game 1–0 (see page 17).

THE GREATEST FINAL?

The 1970 World Cup final is considered to be the greatest ever. Brazil played Italy, and Brazil won the match 4–1. It was an incredible display of attacking football by the Brazil team.

* There were no World Cup tournaments between 1938 and 1950 due to World War II.

◀ Pelé (centre) celebrates with his teammates after winning the 1970 World Cup final against Italy.

HIGHEST SCORING FINAL

The World Cup final in 1958 was played between Brazil and Sweden. Brazil won 5–2 in a thrilling match. Brazil's 17-year-old striker Pelé (see page 26) scored twice in the final.

FONTAINE

Just Fontaine was the star striker for France at the 1958 World Cup, and scored an incredible 13 goals at the tournament. Fontaine's amazing goal-scoring record may never be beaten.

FOOTBALL FACTS

FIFA stands for Fédération Internationale de Football Association. FIFA is the world governing body of football, and is responsible for organizing the World Cup.

▶ The 2010 World Cup final was played between Spain and the Netherlands. Spain won the match 1–0.

G IS FOR...

GERMANY

Germany is one of the most successful countries in the history of the World Cup. As West Germany, the country has won the World Cup on three occasions (in 1954, 1974, and 1990) and appeared in seven finals. Germany's most recent appearance in the final was in 2002, when they were beaten 2–0 by Brazil.

GHOST GOAL

During the match between England and Germany in the second round of the 2010 World Cup, an incident took place that has changed football forever. England midfielder Frank Lampard took a shot from distance. The ball hit the crossbar and bounced down behind the goalkeeper (see below). The ball clearly crossed the goal line, but neither the referee nor his assistant spotted it and the goal was disallowed. Television replays revealed that the ball had bounced a long way behind the goal line. FIFA has decided to allow "goal-line technology" to be used in the 2014 World Cup tournament to prevent this sort of mistake from happening again.

GOLDEN BOOT

At every FIFA World Cup, an award is given out to the player who scores the most goals during the tournament. This award was originally called the "Golden Shoe" but is now called the "Golden Boot". Many great strikers, including Salvatore Schillachi of Italy (1990), Ronaldo of Brazil (2002, see above), and Miroslav Klose of Germany (2006) have received this award.

DID YOU KNOW?

The award for the best performance by an individual player at each World Cup is called the "Golden Ball". Zinedine Zidane (see page 42) won this award for his outstanding performances for France at the 2006 World Cup.

H IS FOR...

HOST COUNTRY

The 20th edition of the FIFA World Cup takes place in Brazil (see below) in 2014 – the second time that Brazil has hosted the tournament. Brazil will join Italy, where the World Cup was played in 1934 and 1990, Germany (1974, 2006), France (1938, 1998), and Mexico (1970, 1986) in becoming World Cup hosts for a second time.

THE 16* COUNTRIES THAT HAVE HOSTED THE WORLD CUP	
ARGENTINA	1978
BRAZIL	1950, 2014
CHILE	1962
ENGLAND	1966
FRANCE	1938, 1998
GERMANY	1974, 2006
ITALY	1934, 1990
JAPAN/ SOUTH KOREA	2002
MEXICO	1970, 1986
SPAIN	1982
SOUTH AFRICA	2010
SWEDEN	1958
SWITZERLAND	1954
URUGUAY	1930
USA	1994

*Japan and South Korea co-hosted the 2002 World Cup.

I IS FOR...

INIESTA

Andrés Iniesta (seen celebrating below) scored the winning goal in the final of the 2010 World Cup in South Africa. The brilliant, skilful midfielder secured victory for Spain against the Netherlands with only a few minutes left in the match. Iniesta was cool and calm as he placed his shot past Maarten Stekelenburg and scored the most important goal in Spain's World Cup history.

ITALY

Italy has a proud World Cup record and has only missed out on two tournaments, in 1930 and 1958. The country has won four World Cup trophies, and the most recent success came in 2006 when it beat France in a penalty shoot-out. Many great Italian players have appeared at the World Cup since the country's first appearance in 1934, including Giuseppe Meazza, Paulo Rossi, and Roberto Baggio.

J IS FOR...

JAIRZINHO

Jairzinho played for Brazil at three World
Cup tournaments, from 1966 to 1974. He was
a fantastic footballer and a crucial member of
the winning Brazilian team at the 1970 World
Cup. During the 1970 World Cup, Jairzinho set
a record for scoring in every one of Brazil's
matches, including the final. This record has
never been equalled.

▼ Jairzinho (far right) in action against
Italy during the 1970 World cup final
in Mexico City, Mexico.

JULES RIMET (1873-1956)

Jules Rimet (see above, left) is one of the most important people in the history of the World Cup. He was FIFA president during the first ever World Cup, and remained in this role until 1954. Jules Rimet was part of a group of men who established the World Cup as a football tournament, and oversaw its early development into an extremely popular sporting event. He became honorary FIFA president in 1954.

TROPHY NAMED IN HIS HONOUR

The World Cup trophy that was created in 1930 was renamed the Jules Rimet Cup in 1946 in honour of the great man. The trophy certainly had an eventful life! It was kept hidden under a bed during World War II to prevent it being confiscated. During the 1966 World Cup in England, the trophy was stolen, only to be discovered a week later by a dog named Pickles! Then in 1983 it was again stolen, but this time it was never returned. The Brazilian Football Association created a replica to replace it.

DID YOU KNOW?

Brazil was allowed to keep the Jules Rimet Cup after winning it for the third time in 1970.

K IS FOR...

KLOSE

Miroslav Klose is a German striker who has played at every World Cup since 2002. In total, Miroslav Klose has played 19 World Cup matches and scored 14 goals.

▼ Miroslav Klose (right) scores a second goal for Germany during a group match at the 2010 World Cup in South Africa.

KOREA

South Korea made its World Cup debut in 1986 and the country has played at every tournament since then. North Korea first played at the World Cup in 1954 and qualified again 12 years later. The two neighbouring nations have had mixed results in the competition.

NORTH KOREA

North Korea's only other appearance after 1966 came in 2010, when they lost all three of their group matches – including a 7–0 thrashing by Portugal. This was in contrast to their promising debut in 1966, when they lost against the Soviet Union, drew with Chile, and beat Italy 1–0 (see page 33), to reach the quarter-final against Portugal. After leading the match 3–0, North Korea lost 5–3 to a very good Portuguese team.

SOUTH KOREA

South Korea has a good record at the World Cup, and the country co-hosted the tournament in 2002 with Japan. South Korea's result at the 2002 World Cup is the best by an Asian country in the history of the competition. The team reached the semi-final, and lost 1–0 against Germany in a close match.

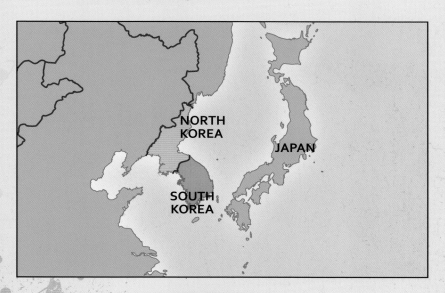

L IS FOR...

LATVIA, LEBANON, LIBERIA...

In the history of the FIFA World Cup, no country that begins with an "L" has ever played in the tournament. This is an unusual record, and the countries on the list below will be hoping that they can qualify for the next World Cup and have the honour of being the first:

Laos, Latvia, Lebanon, Lesotho, Liberia, Libya, Liechtenstein, Lithuania, Luxembourg.

M IS FOR...

MARACANA

The Maracana Stadium in Rio de Janeiro, Brazil is one of the most famous football stadiums in the world. The Maracana has been completely rebuilt for the 2014 World Cup, and will be the venue for seven matches during the tournament, including the final.

DID YOU KNOW?

In 2014 the Maracana Stadium will host the World Cup final for the second time in its history. It will join the Azteca Stadium as the only other venue to have hosted more than one World Cup final match.

FOOTBALL FACTS

Only two footballers have appeared for their country at five World Cup tournaments. The most well known is Lothar Matthäus who played for West Germany at five World Cup tournaments in a row between 1982 and 1998. In total, Matthäus played in 25 World Cup matches for West Germany, including when they won the trophy in 1990. Mexican goalkeeper Antonio Carbajal played in at least one match at every World Cup between 1950 and 1966.

MARADONA

Diego Maradona played for Argentina at four World Cup competitions, where he made a total of 21 appearances and scored eight goals. Maradona led his team to the final of the World Cup on two occasions: in 1986, when they won the trophy, and in 1990, when they were runner-up.

▼ Maradona (centre) in action in 1990, with Germans Lothar Matthäus (right) and Rudi Völler.

MASCOTS

Every World Cup since 1966 has had a mascot. These characters are often based on animals, and have included World Cup Willie (1966) who was based on a lion and Footix (1998) who looked like a cockerel. The 2014 World Cup mascot is called Fuleco and is based on an armadillo.

▲ Winston Reid of New Zealand with his eyes on the ball at the 2010 World Cup.

N IS FOR...

NEW ZEALAND

New Zealand was very unlucky at the 2010 World Cup in South Africa. The team was not expected to cause any surprises at the tournament, which was only their second appearance since playing at the 1982 World Cup. In 1982 they conceded 12 goals and lost all of their matches.

UNUSUAL RESULT

In 2010 New Zealand played three matches in the group stage, against Slovakia, Italy, and Paraguay, and managed to get a draw in all three matches. Despite not losing a single match, New Zealand was knocked out of the competition. This is very unusual, and New Zealand was extremely unlucky to exit the competition.

O IS FOR...

ONLY ONE WORLD CUP APPEARANCE

Many countries from around the world have a long history of playing and succeeding in the World Cup. France, Germany, Brazil, and Argentina are just some of the teams that have qualified for most World Cup tournaments. Other countries have only qualified to play in the World Cup on one occasion. On the right is a list of those 16 countries.

▼ Richmond Forson (right) of Togo in action against France. Togo made their only appearance at a World Cup in 2006. They lost all their group games and scored only one goal.

CUBA	1938
DUTCH EAST INDIES	1938
ISRAEL	1970
HAITI	1974
ZAIRE (now Democratic Republic of Congo)	1974
KUWAIT	1982
IRAQ	1986
CANADA	1986
UNITED ARAB EMIRATES	1990
JAMAICA	1998
CHINA	2002
ANGOLA	2006
TOGO	2006
TRINIDAD AND TOBAGO	2006
SENEGAL	2002
SLOVAKIA	2010

P IS FOR...

PELÉ

Perhaps the greatest footballer ever, Pelé was the star performer for Brazil when they won the World Cup in 1958 and 1970. Pelé was a brilliant goalscorer but he was also an excellent all-round footballer and was able to pass, shoot, and head the ball as well as any other player – if not better! Pelé played for Brazil at four World Cups in a row between 1958 and 1970. In total, he made 14 appearances and scored 12 goals.

PENALTIES

When the World Cup group stage is finished, the tournament becomes a knock-out competition. If any of the matches at this stage ends in a draw after extra time, the two teams involved have to play a penalty shoot-out. The winner of the penalty shoot-out wins the match. The team that scores the most penalties wins. This is a cruel way for a team to exit the World Cup, but it is also an incredible achievement for the team that wins.

DID YOU KNOW?

Only two World Cup finals have ever been decided by a penalty shoot-out. Italy has been involved on both occasions – against Brazil in 1994 and against France in 2006.

▶ Italy's star player Roberto Baggio is devastated after missing a penalty in the 1994 final against Brazil.

PLATINI

Michel Platini (see above) played for France at three World Cups from 1978 to 1986. Platini played in 14 matches at the World Cup, and he has an impressive goal-scoring record for a midfield player, with five goals.

POLL

Englishman Graham Poll was an experienced referee when he was asked to take part in the 2006 World Cup. Unfortunately Poll became famous for all the wrong reasons when he made the mistake of showing a yellow card to the same player three times. He has never refereed another World Cup match.

Q IS FOR...

QATAR

Qatar won the race to host the World Cup in 2022. The country beat off strong competition from the United States and Australia to win the bid to host the prestigious tournament.

QATAR: A FOOTBALL HISTORY...

Qatar has never qualified to play at the World Cup. By hosting the competition, the Qatari national team automatically qualifies to play in the 2022 tournament.

DID YOU KNOW?

Qatar is the smallest country ever to host the World Cup. The next smallest is Switzerland, which is nearly four times the size of Qatar. Switzerland hosted the competition in 1954, when only 16 teams took part.

This map shows where Qatar is, as well as the surrounding countries.

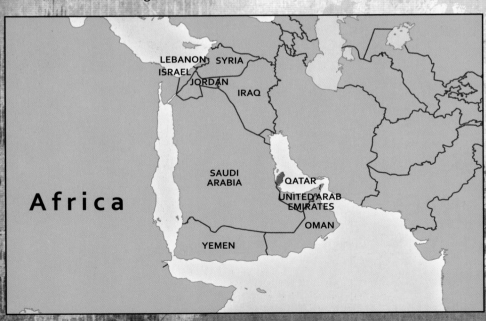

DID YOU KNOW?

Outdoor temperatures in Qatar can reach up to 41° C (106° F). The new stadiums being constructed for the World Cup will have built-in air-conditioning systems to keep the players and spectators cool during matches.

WHERE IS QATAR?

Situated in the Middle East region, Qatar covers an area of only 11,437 square kilometres (4,416 square miles) and has a population of just 1.9 million people. It will be a remarkable achievement if this small country can successfully host the World Cup in 2022. Qatar will have to cope with the influx of all of the other teams, plus thousands of football fans from around the world.

R IS FOR...

RED CARD

Players who repeatedly break the rules or commit a serious foul during a match are shown different coloured cards to signify the seriousness of the offence. A yellow card acts as a warning, and a red card means that the player must leave the field of play. Two yellow cards will automatically lead to a red card.

RED CARD FACTS

Here are some more facts about red cards:

- The first player to be shown a red card and sent off in a World Cup match was Peru's Mario de las Casas, during the 1930 World Cup.

- The first player to be shown a red card in the World Cup final was Pedro Monzón of Argentina in 1990. Since then four more players have been sent off in the final match, including the Netherlands' John Heitinga in 2010.

- The match with the highest number of red cards in World Cup history took place in 2006 when the Netherlands and Portugal both had two players sent off in the same match.

RUSSIA

Russia beat off strong competition from other countries, including England, to win the race to host the World Cup in 2018. Formerly known as the Soviet Union, Russia made their debut in the 1958 competition in Sweden, and has appeared in nine World Cups in total. Russia's best finish at a World Cup came in 1966, when they reached the semi-final.

WHERE IS RUSSIA?

Russia is the largest country in the world, covering an area of 17,000,000 square kilometres (6.6 million square miles) and with a population of almost 143 million people. Russia is so huge that it stretches across two continents: Europe and Asia.

▲ The Soviet Union (in red) playing Portugal at the 1966 World Cup at Wembley Stadium.

S IS FOR...

SALENKO

Oleg Salenko played for Russia at the 1994 World Cup tournament in the United States. Salenko set a new World Cup goal-scoring record during the tournament when he scored five goals in Russia's 6–1 defeat of Cameroon. His record has not been matched since.

SEPP BLATTER

Sepp Blatter (see below) is the president of FIFA. He was voted in as president in 1998 and has been in the role during the last four World Cups. Swiss-born Blatter is a very controversial character, and has made some outrageous comments in public. He has also been accused of corruption on more than one occasion.

▲ The Cameroon players couldn't believe it when they beat the defending world champions Argentina 1–0 at a 1990 World Cup match in Italy! François Omam-Biyik scored the goal.

SHOCK RESULTS

- The opening match in 2002 caused a shock when defending champions France lost 1–0 to World Cup newcomers, Senegal.

- In 1950 the United States beat England at the World Cup in Brazil. This surprising result sent shockwaves all around the world – until Uruguay surprisingly beat the host nation Brazil 2–1 in the final!

- Italy has twice failed to beat teams from the Korean peninsula and been knocked out of the World Cup. The first time was in 1966 when they were shocked by North Korea, and they were also beaten by South Korea in the 2002 World Cup.

T IS FOR...

TROPHY

The famous and instantly recognizable World Cup trophy was first handed to the World Cup winners at the 1974 tournament. The trophy replaced the Jules Rimet Cup (see page 19) after Brazil was allowed to keep the original trophy as winners of three World Cups.

WORLD CUP TROPHY: THE FACTS

- It is 36 cm high and made out of 18-carat gold.
- The bands near the bottom are made of malachite, a semi-precious metal.
- The names of all the winners since 1974 have been engraved on the underside of the trophy.
- It was designed by Italian artist Silvio Gazzaniga.

U IS FOR...

URUGUAY

Uruguay has been associated with the FIFA World Cup ever since the tournament began in 1930. The first World Cup was hosted by Uruguay, and they won the competition, beating Argentina 4–2 in the final (see below).

WHERE IS URUGUAY?

Uruguay is a small country in South America with a population of around 3.5 million people.

TWO-TIME WORLD CHAMPIONS

In 1930 Uruguay became the first football world champions, and they managed to repeat this feat in Brazil in 1950. They were the underdogs going into the final with the host country, and the stadium was packed with fanatical Brazilian fans. Uruguay pulled off one of the greatest shock results in World Cup history to win the match 2–1.

BRAZIL

BOLIVIA

PARAGUAY

CHILE

URUGUAY

ARGENTINA

ATLANTIC OCEAN

DID YOU KNOW?

Uruguay is level with Argentina on the World Cup winners' list. Only Germany, Italy, and Brazil have won more tournaments (see page 39).

V IS FOR...

VALDERRAMA

During the 1990s Carlos Valderrama was one of the most famous footballers in the world. Colombia's greatest ever player appeared for his country at three World Cups in a row between 1990 and 1998. Valderrama helped Colombia to their best finish at the tournament, when they reached the second round in Italy in 1990.

DID YOU KNOW?

Valderrama's hairstyle made him instantly recognizable. His big hair meant you couldn't miss him when he played!

VENEZUELA

Venezuela has never qualified for the World Cup. They are the only major country from South America that has never played in the tournament. However, there has been a lot of investment in football in Venezuela over the past 20 years, and the country is determined to qualify for the next World Cup.

VUVUZELA

The vuvuzela became a very popular fan accessory at the 2010 World Cup in South Africa. The brightly coloured, long plastic horns can be blown to create an unusual sound. Many thousands of fans at the 2010 World Cup bought vuvuzelas, and the noise when they were all blown together became one of the most memorable sounds of the World Cup in South Africa.

FOOTBALL FACTS

The following South American teams have all played at the World Cup:

Argentina, Bolivia, Brazil, Chile, Colombia, Ecuador, Paraguay, Peru, Uruguay

DID YOU KNOW?

The noise made by the vuvuzelas was so loud that FIFA considered banning the blowing of the horns during matches!

W IS FOR...

WEMBLEY STADIUM

The historic and famous Wembley Stadium in London
was rebuilt at the start of the 21st century. Long before it
was totally redesigned and rebuilt, Wembley Stadium was
the venue for the 1966 World Cup final. More than 96,000
people watched England and West Germany battle it out
for the trophy.

FANTASTIC FINAL

It was a great final, full of goals – plus a controversial moment,
when a shot by England was judged to have crossed the goal
line. England thought they had won the match 2–1 in regulation
time, but a late goal from West Germany in the 89th minute
meant that the huge Wembley crowd was able to enjoy an extra
30 minutes of World Cup final football. England won the match
4–2 after extra time.

FOOTBALL FACTS

World Cup wins:

Brazil – 5
Italy – 4
Germany – 3
Argentina – 2
Uruguay – 2
England – 1
France – 1
Spain – 1

WORLD CUP WINNERS

The 2014 World Cup will be the 20th edition of the world famous football tournament. The most successful team in the history of the World Cup is Brazil, which has won the World Cup on five occasions. The second most successful team in history is Italy which has won the tournament four times.

X IS FOR...

XAVI AND XABI

Spain's midfield stars Xavi Hernandez (see above, left) and Xabi Alonso (right) played an important role in helping Spain to win their first World Cup in 2010. They combined with the other members of their team to produce some excellent football that was applauded by fans all over the world. These two players in particular helped Spain to keep possession of the ball during difficult matches, and also created chances for teammates to score.

DID YOU KNOW?

Lev Yashin (see opposite) has the honour of being the only goalkeeper to be named European Footballer of the Year. He received the award in recognition of his consistently outstanding performances.

Y IS FOR...

YASHIN

Lev Yashin was the goalkeeper for the Soviet Union at three World Cup tournaments, from 1958 to 1966. He was an incredible player and had all the major attributes of a great goalkeeper: agility, good positioning, and strong hands. Yashin combined his talents brilliantly during his career and is considered to be one of the greatest goalkeepers of all time.

The best goalkeeper at every World Cup is given a prestigious award in recognition of their excellent play. This award is named after Lev Yashin. Here is a list of the winners of the Lev Yashin award at the most recent World Cup tournaments:

2010	Iker Casillas (Spain)
2006	Gianluigi Buffon (Italy)
2002	Oliver Kahn (Germany)
1998	Fabien Barthez (France)
1994	Michel Preud'homme (Belgium)

In 2010, the award was renamed the "Golden Glove".

Z IS FOR...

ZIDANE

In 1998 Zinedine Zidane guided the French team all the way to the final of the World Cup, where they beat Brazil 3–0. Zidane was voted Man of the Match after heading two goals that helped his team win the World Cup for the first time in their history.

A GLITTERING CAREER

Zidane played for France at three World Cups, and reached the final on two occasions. He left his mark on the tournament in 1998 by scoring in the final. In 2002 he was injured, and unable to help France get out of the group stage. In 2006 Zidane was given the Golden Ball award (see page 15) for his fantastic performance in leading his team to their second World Cup final.

▼ Zinedine Zidane celebrates after scoring a goal in the 1998 World Cup final.

Zidane had incredible skill and passing ability, and scored some wonderful goals during his career. Zidane won trophies whoever he played for. He won the league title in Italy, twice with Juventus, and once in Spain with Real Madrid. Zidane also won the UEFA Champions League when he was playing for Real Madrid.

UNFORTUNATE ENDING

After his success at the 1998 World Cup, Zidane's career ended on a bad note when he was sent off in the final of the 2006 World Cup. During extra time, Zidane was seen to headbutt an Italian opponent in the chest. The referee had no option but to show Zidane the red card. It was a very disappointing end to a glorious football career.

▲ Legendary Spain goalkeeper Andoni Zubizarreta attempts to make a save.

ZUBIZARRETA

Andoni Zubizarreta is a Spanish football legend, and was Spain's goalkeeper in four World Cup competitions, between 1986 and 1998. In total, Zubizarreta played in 16 World Cup matches.

GLOSSARY

agility able to move quickly and easily

continent one of the world's largest land masses. There are seven continents on Earth.

confiscate take something away from someone

controversial something that is likely to cause people to have strong opinions and disagree about it

corruption dishonest behaviour by someone in authority

counter-attack attack made in response to another attack

Czechoslovakia country in Eastern Europe that separated into Slovakia and the Czech Republic in 1993

debut someone making their first appearance. For example, a footballer playing at the World Cup for the first time is making their debut.

extra time extra period of play that is added to a football match if it is a draw at the end of regulation time (90 minutes). Extra time lasts for 30 minutes, with two halves of 15 minutes.

goal-line technology technology that can prove whether the ball has crossed the goal line

hat-trick when a player scores three goals in one match it is called a "hat-trick"

knock-out competition in a knock-out competition, the winner of the match goes through to the next round and the loser is "knocked out" of the competition

legend famous person who is known for their particular talent or success

penalty shoot-out after extra time, if the score is still level, the two teams pick five players to try and score five penalties. The team that scores the most penalties wins.

prestigious something that is very important or special

underdog person or team in a contest that is expected to lose

West Germany between 1945 and 1990 Germany was split into West Germany and East Germany

FIND OUT MORE

BOOKS

Defender (Football Files), Michael Hurley (Raintree, 2011)

Fantastic Football, Clive Gifford (Oxford University Press, 2010)

Goalkeeper (Football Files), Michael Hurley (Raintree, 2011)

Midfielder (Football Files), Michael Hurley (Raintree, 2011)

Soccer (DK: Eyewitness Books), Hugh Hornby (DK Publishing, 2010)

Steven Gerrard (World Cup Heroes), Adam Cottier (John Blake Publishing, 2010

Striker (Football Files), Michael Hurley (Raintree, 2011)

The Kingfisher Football Encyclopaedia, Clive Gifford (Kingfisher, 2010)

Wayne Rooney (World Cup Heroes), Adam Cottier (John Blake Publishing, 2010

World Cup 2014 (World Cup Fever), Michael Hurley (Raintree, 2014)

World Cup Heroes (World Cup Fever), Michael Hurley (Raintree, 2014)

World Cup Nations (World Cup Fever), Michael Hurley (Raintree, 2014)

WEBSITES

www.fifa.com
The official website for everything World Cup related. You can find the latest team and player news, fixtures, results, and photos from World Cup matches.

en.mascot.fifa.com
Follow Fuleco, the official mascot for the World Cup in Brazil. Catch up on the latest news, play games, and check out the latest photos of Fuleco as he spreads the word about the biggest football tournament in the world.

www.fifa.com/worldcup/archive/index.html
This is a great place to start if you want to find out facts and stats from previous World Cups. You can find stats from every match played and goals scored at all of the World Cup tournaments.

www.fifa.com/classicfootball/index.html?intcmp=fifacom_hp_module_classic_football
Check out match reports on important World Cup matches from the past, and find out more about some of the greatest ever footballers, football clubs, and stadiums around the world.

www.footballworldcupbrazil2014.com/
This unofficial guide to the 2014 World Cup provides videos, blogs, team profiles, and facts and figures about previous World Cup tournaments.

kids.nationalgeographic.co.uk/kids/places/find/brazil/
If you want to know more about Brazil and the history, geography, and culture of the country this is a great place to start.

LOOK IT UP...

1. In the history of the World Cup there have only been two people who have won the tournament as a player and manager for their country. Can you find out who they are?

2. S is for ... Soccer City. Soccer City is the football stadium in Johannesburg where the final of the 2010 World Cup was played. Do you know or can you find out where previous World Cup finals have been played?

3. Fans and the media often give nicknames to players who stand out. Former Italy player Roberto Baggio was given the nickname "The Divine Ponytail" because of his incredible football skills and his hairstyle. Do you know of, or, can you find out about any other famous players who have been given nicknames?

4. H is for ... hat-tricks. A player scoring a hat-trick, or three goals, is quite a rare event at the World Cup. For a player to score more than one hat-trick is very unusual. Do you know, or can you find out which players have scored more than one hat-trick in World Cup history?

INDEX